Numeracy

DEVELOPING ADULT TEACHING AND LEARNING: PRACTITIONER GUIDES

Jon Swain, Barbara Newmarch and Oonagh Gormley

promoting adult learning

(England and Wales)
21 De Montfort Street
Leicester LE1 7GE

Company registration no. 2603322
Charity registration no. 1002775
Published by NIACE in association with NRDC.

NIACE has a broad remit to promote lifelong learning opportunities for adults.
NIACE works to develop increased participation in education and training,
particularly for those who do not have easy access because of class, gender, age,
race, language and culture, learning difficulties or disabilities, or insufficient
financial resources.

For a full catalogue of all NIACE's publications visit
www.niace.org.uk/publications

Cataloguing in Publications Data
A CIP record for this title is available from the British Library
ISBN 978-1-86201-337-7

Cover design by Creative by Design Limited, Paisley
Designed and typeset by Creative by Design Limited, Paisley
Printed and bound by Aspect Binders and Print Ltd

Developing adult teaching and learning: Practitioner guides

This is one of several linked publications arising from the five Effective Practice Studies carried out by the National Research and Development Centre for Adult Literacy and Numeracy (NRDC) from 2003 to 2007.

The five studies explored effective teaching and learning in reading, writing, numeracy, ESOL and using ICT. To date, three series of publications have been produced from the Effective Practice Studies: the research reports and the development project reports, all published by NRDC; and these practitioner guides, published in partnership between NIACE and NRDC.

For more information on the first two series, please see **www.nrdc.org.uk**

Contents

Acknowledgements

We are grateful to the following practitioners who peer reviewed an earlier draft of this guide:

- Deborah Holder
- Cathy Magee
- Ann McDonnell
- Sue Neiduszynska

About this guide

The aim of this guide is to update teachers on research about teaching numeracy and to encourage them to reflect on their practice. It is not a manual on how to teach numeracy, but by giving a few examples, we hope to inspire teachers to try out ideas and approaches which research suggests are effective.

In particular:

■ it has been written for teachers working with adults and young people in adult numeracy and maths provision;

■ it draws on findings of a research study on effective practice in numeracy (Coben *et al.*, 2007) undertaken by the National Research and Development Centre for adult literacy and numeracy (NRDC). It also draws on research within the Maths4Life project *Thinking Through Mathematics* (Swain and Swan, 2007), as well as wider research into teaching and learning mathematics which underpins these approaches (Swan, 2006);

■ we have attempted to unpick the implications of the research findings in a very practical way. The guide has been written by teachers and researchers working together, and is highly relevant to the classroom;

■ it does not cover all aspects of teaching numeracy, but considers a number of themes and issues to stimulate thinking; and

■ it challenges teachers to ask questions and undertake their own classroom research in order to understand how best to help their learners develop their mathematics skills.

Teachers who are interested to learn more about the nature of the research and its findings are encouraged to read the full version, or the summary report, of *Effective Teaching and Learning: Numeracy* (Coben *et al.*, 2006). The following reading is also recommended: *Thinking Through Mathematics: Research Report* (Swain and Swan, 2007), *Collaborative Learning in Mathematics: A Challenge to our Beliefs and Practices* (Swan, 2006) and *'Beyond the Daily Application': Making Numeracy Teaching Meaningful to Adult Learners* (Swain *et al.*, 2005).

Note: There is a tendency in official documents to treat the terms numeracy and mathematics as interchangeable, and in this guide we also use them in a similar fashion.

1 | **From research to practice**

The Effective Practice project

Background

The Effective Teaching and Learning Numeracy project (Effective Practice) (Coben *et al.*, 2007) began in August 2003 and was completed in March 2006. The project investigated approaches to the teaching of numeracy, aiming to identify the extent of learners' progress, and to establish correlations between learners' progress and the strategies and practices used by teachers.

The study involved 412 learners and 34 teachers in 47 classes across a range of contexts. Forty percent of the learners were 16–19 year-olds. Classes were observed between one and four times during each course; 250 learners were assessed at two time points and 243 completed attitude surveys. Background information was collected on teachers and learners, and interviews were carried out with 33 teachers and 112 learners.

Main findings

- Although there was significant progress, with an average gain of 9 per cent in test scores, there were few relationships between observed teaching practice and learning or attitude gains.

- Adult numeracy classes have a huge diversity of learners in terms of, for example, learner ages, abilities, dispositions, purposes and aspiration within a great variety of settings.

- Over 90 per cent of learners interviewed expressed a high level of satisfaction with their course and their teacher. Learners were usually highly engaged.

- Teachers valued 'flexibility' as a key feature of effective practice. They appeared to adapt to their circumstances and respond to learners' needs.

- The heterogeneous nature of adult numeracy teaching, and the number of variables amongst teachers and learners, make it difficult to produce findings that can be generalised across the whole sector.

Learners' attitudes and the reasons they attend numeracy classes

Attitudes

Many learners come to classes with a poor experience of learning maths at school. Some had fallen behind and 'switched off' from learning.

> If you didn't understand something in maths class it was just all crosses instead of ticks. And then the next subject was moved on so there was no time to go back and help really.

"...initial anxiety about joining a numeracy class can soon translate into positive attitudes..."

The Effective Practice research found that learners feel more confident about mathematics once they start a course. Given this, it is important to acknowledge that initial anxiety about joining a numeracy class can soon translate into positive attitudes and raise levels of confidence and self-esteem.

> Vicky has made me feel so confident about maths. I've never felt so good about maths, and for the first time ever I can now say I enjoy maths. And that's quite a new, big, thing for me.

Clearly, the first few sessions will be important in getting started on this journey, and careful attention to setting the scene in terms of classroom ethos, teacher expectations and the learning process will be critical. Once learners begin to understand and succeed they will want to learn more.

> Like when you see maths, and to be able to do it, it makes me so proud. I am going somewhere and I want to do more.

Motivations

Research has established that learners' motivations for joining numeracy classes are many, intricate and often overlap. Most learners reported 'getting a qualification' as the main reason for doing a numeracy course, with 'getting a better job' being the second most popular response. While supporting children is another very common reason, it was not so important in this research because over 40 per cent of the sample were 16–19 year-olds and so would not have children of school age. In common with other research findings, these data also confirm that many learners regard success in mathematics as a signifier of intelligence, and they want to prove that they can achieve in a high status subject.

> I feel equal, when I'm at work now I don't still feel that I'm a second rate person anymore. I don't feel that I have to prove myself anymore.

It is often assumed that people attend numeracy courses to help them function more effectively in the outside world. Our research, however, suggests that this was perceived by learners as being a comparatively minor reason.

> *It hasn't been the daily application that has caught me, has got me so ... it's beyond the daily application, it's so exciting and I don't think you do have to make it daily, practical, mundane. It doesn't have to be just practical.*

Common forms of practice

The study suggests that the dominant mode of teaching numeracy to adults remains one of transmission where teachers show learners procedures, break concepts down into smaller parts and demonstrate examples. The most common form of organisation tends to be whole-class exposition followed by learners working individually through worksheets, and there is little group or collaborative work. Thus the dominant mode of teaching is typified by the 'triple X' teacher who starts the session by giving learners 'explanations', continues by 'works through examples' and then asks learners to 'practice exercises'.

What teachers are doing well

The research found that teachers generally:

- have adequate subject knowledge;
- give clear explanations;
- give learners time to gain understanding;
- provide a variety of learning activities;
- are enthusiastic;
- give learners praise and encouragement;
- monitor learning and give learners feedback; and
- give opportunities for learners to express themselves.

What teachers need to develop

In general, teachers need to:

- use more 'higher order' questions to probe learners' mistakes and misconceptions;
- challenge learners and encourage higher-level thinking;
- relate or connect other mathematical topics to each other;

- place a higher emphasis on conceptual understanding;
- ask learners to engage in more problem-solving activities;
- make greater use of discussion groups and collaborative learning;
- make greater use of calculators and ICT; and
- use more concrete materials/resources to aid understanding.

The importance of subject-specific pedagogy

Both the Effective Practice and the Thinking Through Mathematics (TTM) projects make a distinction between teachers' *mathematical knowledge*, which concerns the content, and teachers' *subject-specific pedagogical knowledge*, which refers to how to teach mathematics to learners.

Some teachers have received little professional development which addresses this issue and rely on methods that they were taught when they were at school.

I'd been taught to sit up straight and pay attention and very much chalk talk and textbook and that's the way it had been done for me and that's what I brought with me.

Teachers need to know how learners might come to understand mathematics and then be able to offer teaching strategies that facilitate further learning. They are continually telling researchers that they need more help from initial teacher training and professional development to build up a repertoire of ideas and activities.

It is something you really struggle with, with knowing how to approach it.

Implications for professional development

Research into numeracy/mathematics conducted by NRDC has produced a set of implications for continuing professional development (CPD) and initial teacher training (Swain and Swan, 2007). Used in conjuction with TTM and other resources produced by Maths4Life, these are rich resources to draw on for professional development activity.

Implications for policy makers and managers

One of the main recommendations is to facilitate iterative models of collaborative professional development where teachers:

- trial ideas, materials, strategies and teaching approaches in the classroom;

- return as a group to report back, reflect on and evaluate them; and

- then return to the classroom to retrial them in the light of these new perceptions/experiences.

The research shows beneficial effects of introducing formalised peer observations and their role as an essential feature of CPD.

Implications for teacher educators in continuing professional development

Professional development should include significant content on teaching the basic concepts:

- subject-specific pedagogy;

- strategies in classroom management and collaborative organisation;

- techniques of formative assessment; and

- strategies for recognising and dealing with learners' misconceptions and discussions on the issue of differentiation.

The research-informed resources produced through Maths4Life offer tools for use by teacher educators in CPD activity.

2 Features of 'good' or 'effective' practice

What the teachers told us from the Effective Practice project

Teachers described their classes, and researchers drew out the following features of what the teachers suggested an effective session should involve:

- Being flexible and able to use a variety of approaches to accommodate learners' needs.
- Enabling learners to make connections to other areas of mathematics.
- Good planning, including anticipating learners' responses.
- Starting from where the learners are, providing a variety of activities, and a variety of ways of doing things that incorporate learners' own methods.
- Extending learners beyond their comfort zone:

  It is about starting from where the learners are, be aware of that, and pushing them on and extending them, as far as they are comfortable going, probably a bit further.

- Getting learners to interact, and viewing learning as a social activity.
- Encouraging learners to make their thinking explicit to the teacher and to other learners; allowing them to articulate what they understand.

Learners' perceptions of what makes a good numeracy teacher

Learners recognise that the role of the teacher is crucial:

If you don't like the teacher, you ain't going to learn nothing.

Researchers asked the learners what they thought makes a good teacher. In order of frequency, a good teacher was described as someone who:

- has good communication skills; explains things clearly using several different ways, including breaking down concepts into small steps;
- has good relations with, and respects, learners; does not make them feel stupid; is approachable and listens carefully to their needs;

- makes maths interesting by being imaginative and makes sure there is plenty of variety in each session. Does not lecture and talk too much;
- gives individual help;
- does not rush through the work; and
- has a firm grasp of their subject.

Learners also wanted a teacher who was patient, cheerful, had a sense of humour, was relaxed and easy-going, and made them feel welcome.

Further research evidence

The extensive research carried out by NRDC is beginning to build a picture of what 'effective' or 'good' practice might actually look like. TTM builds on many years of research in the further education sector, and draws on the work of an earlier project by the Department for Education and Skills' (DfES) Standards Unit in 2005, 'Improving Learning in Mathematics'. Both these projects trialled and evaluated a set of teaching principles developed by Malcolm Swan with learners working from Entry 1 to 3. The 'approaches' to teaching and learning have recently received very favourable comments from Ofsted (see the following section), and the eight principles are set out below. The approaches are used in conjunction with a pack of materials/resources which can be ordered free of charge at **http://www.Maths4Life.org**.

For more information, see the report of the TTM project (Swain and Swan, 2007).

Teaching is more effective when it ...

builds on the knowledge learners already have.	This means developing formative assessment techniques and adapting our teaching to accommodate individual learning needs (Black and Wiliam, 1998).
exposes and discusses common misconceptions.	Learning activities should expose current thinking, create 'tensions' by confronting learners with inconsistencies, and allow opportunities for resolution through discussion (Askew and Wiliam, 1995).
uses higher-order questions.	Questioning is more effective when it promotes explanation, application and synthesis rather than mere recall (Askew and Wiliam, 1995).

"Learners wanted a teacher who was patient, cheerful, had a sense of humour, was relaxed and easy-going, and made them feel welcome."

uses co-operative small-group work.	Activities are more effective when they encourage critical, constructive discussion, rather than argumentation or uncritical acceptance (Mercer, 2000). Shared goals and group accountability are important (Askew and Wiliam, 1995).
encourages reasoning rather than 'answer getting'.	Often, learners are more concerned with what they have 'done' than with what they have learned. It is better to aim for depth than for superficial 'coverage'.
uses rich, collaborative tasks.	The tasks we use should be accessible, extendable, encourage decision-making, promote discussion, encourage creativity, and encourage 'what if' and 'what if not?' questions (Ahmed, 1987).
creates connections between topics.	Learners often find it difficult to generalise and transfer their learning to other topics and contexts. Related concepts (such as division, fraction and ratio) remain unconnected. Effective teachers build bridges between ideas (Askew *et al.*, 1997).
uses technology.	Computers and interactive whiteboards allow us to present concepts in visual, dynamic and exciting ways that motivate learners.

What inspectors are beginning to say

"Students were challenged to think for themselves, encouraged to discuss problems and to work collaboratively."

Senior managers are more likely to be persuaded to introduce at least some of the approaches proposed by TTM if they see that the other organisations that are implementing them are achieving grade 1 inspection results.

In its 'key findings', the Ofsted report, *Evaluating Mathematics Provision for 14–19 year-olds* (2006), quotes that a specific factor that contributes to raising learners' achievement is the effective use of 'high quality learning resources, including new resources devised by the Standards Unit in the DfES' (p. 2). Many principles that the Ofsted report recommends should be used to raise achievement in mathematics are striking in their similarity to the principles advocated in TTM:

The best teaching gave a strong sense of the coherence of mathematical ideas; it focused on understanding mathematical concepts and developed critical thinking and reasoning. Careful questioning identified misconceptions and helped to resolve them, and positive use was made of incorrect answers to develop understanding and to encourage students to contribute. Students were challenged to think for themselves, encouraged to discuss problems and to work collaboratively. Effective use was made of information and communication technology (ICT). In contrast, teaching which presented mathematics as a collection of arbitrary rules and provided a narrow range of learning activities did not motivate students and limited their achievement. Focusing heavily on examination questions enabled students to pass examinations, but did not necessarily enable them to apply their knowledge independently in different contexts. (Ofsted, 2006)

3 The teaching process

One of the main findings from the Effective Practice project was that there was no quick recipe for successful/effective practice – learning mathematics takes time. It also showed the limitations of trying to measure effectiveness based on learners' progress measured between two points over a relatively short period of time (the average amount of teaching hours in the Effective Practice project was 39 hours). However, further research in the TTM project strongly suggests that, broadly speaking, practice is most effective when it promotes *active learning*, and when the teacher uses *'connected' and 'challenging' teaching methods.*

Many adult learners appear to view mathematics as a series of disconnected procedures and techniques that must be learned by rote. However, TTM found that when learners engage in discussing and explaining ideas, challenging, and teaching one another, creating and solving each other's questions and working collaboratively to share methods and results, their learning was more robust, transferable and endured over time (see Swan, 2006).

The following sections in this chapter look firstly at the different types of belief systems teachers may have, and then at a number of key principles which we believe constitute effective practice in numeracy classrooms: encouraging active learner participation; planning; building on what learners know; mistakes and misconceptions; organisation of learners; meeting the needs of all learners; assessment and questioning. In summary, the message is that teachers need to think beyond *what* they are going to teach to *how* they are going to teach it, and the learners' likely reactions and responses. Some ideas and activities are offered to exemplify how teachers might incorporate these principles into their own practice.

Teachers' beliefs about mathematics

In general terms, teachers who believe that mathematics is a set of universal truths, which exists 'out there', tend to believe that the way to learn mathematics is to be taught fixed procedures which give access to this particular set of knowledge. Such teachers can be termed 'transmission' teachers of mathematics.

An alternative position is taken by educators who believe that learners should be left to 'discover' mathematical concepts and methods for themselves, with little input from the teacher. This 'discovery' method can have the disadvantage that all methods are equally valued, however inefficient they may be.

Other 'connectionist' teachers believe that learning mathematics is about exploring the interconnected nature of the subject as a more social endeavour, where the learning process is not linear, and where learning comes about through challenging meanings through discussion. Research (Swan, 2006) suggests that the connectionist approach leads to deeper and longer lasting learning in mathematics.

Aspects of these beliefs are summarised in the table below:

	Transmission	Discovery	Connectionist
Mathematics is...	a given body of knowledge and standard procedures. A set of universal truths and rules which need to be conveyed to learners.	a creative subject in which the teacher should take a facilitating role, allowing learners to create their own concepts and methods. Mathematics is a personal construction of the learner.	an interconnected body of ideas and reasoning processes which the teacher and the learner create together through discussion.
Learning is...	an individual activity based on watching, listening and imitating until fluency is attained.	an individual activity based on practical exploration and reflection.	an interpersonal activity in which learners are challenged and arrive at understanding through discussion.

(Continued)

	Transmission	Discovery	Connectionist
Teaching is...	structuring a linear curriculum for the learners; giving verbal explanations and checking that these have been understood through practice questions; correcting misunderstandings when learners fail to 'grasp' what is taught.	assessing when a learner is ready to learn; providing a stimulating environment to facilitate exploration; and avoiding misunderstandings by the careful sequencing of experiences.	a non-linear dialogue between teacher and learners in which meanings and connections are explored verbally. Misunderstandings are made explicit and worked on.

Encouraging active learner participation

Learners come to mathematics classes with clear expectations of the teacher, the mathematics and the ways in which they will be expected to learn. Some may expect that the teacher will spend most of their time talking in front of the class, and many may have previously measured their success in maths by how many worksheets they have completed, or how may ticks they received, rather than by how much their understanding has developed. Some think a classroom is a place where learners do not talk much together, and therefore may find it difficult to adjust to collaborative approaches to learning. Teachers need to discuss with learners the benefits of more interactive teaching and learning approaches, and be explicit about why they believe these are likely to be effective.

Below is an example of how this might be done:

> Amend this set of cards with statements about learning mathematics (opposite) so that they are relevant for your learners. Cut up and give to learners to work on in pairs or small groups. Learners should discuss each card in turn to try and reach a consensus about the statement. They place the card under one of three headings: 'Agree', 'Disagree' or 'Difference of opinion'. The teacher can then discuss with the whole group some of the key points raised.

The teacher should mark all our answers.	Mistakes are learning opportunities.	You should try not to make any mistakes in maths.	It's cheating to work with another person because you can just copy their answers.
We learn more if we mark each other's work.	If you learn all the rules off by heart, you'll be good at maths.	In maths it's really important to understand why you do things.	The most important thing is to get the right answers.
If you practise the same maths rule over and over again you will learn it.	Maths is a language.	It's better to do your maths on your own.	You learn a lot from other students.
Looking at the answers is cheating.	It's a good idea to work backwards from the answers.	Explaining something to someone else helps you understand it better.	You shouldn't argue in a maths class.
The teacher should show you how to do everything on the board.	If people talk in a maths class that means they are not really concentrating on their work.	The more worksheets you can complete the better.	You can learn a lot from games.

Planning

All teachers need to plan for the long term (a scheme of work covering a term or a year), the medium term (a module or topic such as 'data handling'), and the short term (specific sessions). One of the main messages that research shows is that for this planning to be effective, it also needs to be flexible.

Long- and medium-term planning

The core curriculum provides a map of the range of skills and capabilities that learners are expected to need in order to function and progress at work and in society. The document has been subject to a lot of misinterpretation by both teachers and managers, and it is important to emphasise that the curriculum should be seen as a guide and a support, rather than a prescriptive and limiting set of instructions. The then Department for Education and Employment was quite clear that the Adult Numeracy Core Curriculum

> *...is not a series of rigid lesson plans to be taught by every teacher and followed by every learner.* (DfEE, 1999)

A scheme of work for numeracy should also be viewed as a flexible working document which can be adapted according to the changing needs of the group. Its purpose is to give a general overview of the topics to be covered during the time available, and it can be seen as a useful schedule, organising topics in a meaningful way. Although it can be mapped to the core curriculum and reflect the requirements of the accreditation the learners are aiming at, it should not restrict teachers and learners from tackling topics a higher level, if teachers think it is appropriate. One of the side-effects of the core curriculum is that its structure compartmentalises mathematics into discrete topics, and some teachers may tend to plan the order of their teaching according to this conceptual layout.

A scheme of work does not have to be set out in a linear form, and can be used to identify ways of making links between different areas of the curriculum, and integrating different topics. Some teachers in the TTM project felt liberated when they realised that the core curriculum could be interpreted more flexibly.

> *I used to teach, until fairly recently, from topic to topic, I've got the core curriculum here, I know I've got to cover these topics and I'll go through them. I don't do that any more. [I now] combine all these elements together and I think it's wonderful.*

Short-term planning

Thorough planning is essential. Plans need to show an outline of the proposed structure, indicating links with previous work and some detail of the planned range of activities and how these are differentiated. It can be useful to include notes about specific maths language to explain or reinforce. It can be especially important to plan in some detail the key questions that need to be asked. Thinking in advance about these and deciding how and when to ask them provides a powerful focus.

A lesson plan is not set in stone, and a teacher may choose to change things in response to what learners raise, thinking on their feet. Some of the very best sessions happen when teachers create time, in advance of the lesson, to think about *how* they are planning to teach. During the TTM project, one teacher wrote down the main learning areas that he thought were particularly important as an aide-memoire or check list:

Discussion/thinking

Link topics – patterns

Challenge

Conversation style – discussion

Must have beginning and end – GO WITH FLOW

Don't give answers, get learners to think

Solve problems together

Peer learning/exchanging ideas

Learners not afraid to make mistakes

Everyone has different way of learning

If it isn't broke, don't fix it. Whatever works for you as a learner

I will only suggest different strategies to unlock the door

The planning also included trying to anticipate learners' questions so that the teacher could think about his own responses.

Of course not every teacher will be able to spend a lot of time preparing for every session. Each context is different and has its own structural factors, which produces its own constraints. Overall though, and at the risk of repetition, the message is that teachers need to think beyond *what* they are going to teach to *how* they are going to teach it, and the learners' likely reactions and responses.

Building on what learners know

Research suggests (Swan, 2006) that building on the knowledge learners already have leads to more effective teaching. This means teachers need to find ways to uncover this knowledge and understanding, which may be hidden, partial or limited by a particular context.

Formative assessment can be thought of as an activity whose main purpose is to promote learning, whereas *summative assessment* is normally used to measure progress and to evaluate the impact of teaching. One strategy used by some of the teachers in both the Effective Practice and TTM projects was to begin sessions by asking the class to describe what they already knew or understood about a topic. They followed this up with further questions and challenges in order to develop understanding throughout the rest of the session. Their aim is thus a type of formative assessment – treating the beginning of a session as a 'fact-finding' exercise in order to discover both 'firm ground' and also identify learning needs that needed to be followed up. One teacher explained this to the class as follows:

> *Before we start tell me what you know. I'll put that on the whiteboard and that is my starting point. So even if things are down that are not correct, it doesn't matter, we'll put them down and then discuss them.*

An example of this strategy comes from *Collaborative Learning in Mathematics* by Malcolm Swan (2006):

> Chris began one lesson by writing the number 1.43 in the centre of the board and the whole lesson consisted of Chris orally eliciting associations and connections with this number through a series of questions.
>
> ■ How would you say that number?
> ■ Where might you see something like this?

- What might it represent?

- Height, OK. What sort of units?

- So it could be height. 1.43 metres. How high is that?

- Do you know how high you are in metres?

- How big is a metre? Give us a metre. Show me with your arms.

- If you have 1.43 metres – How else might you describe that?

- Is there anything else this number might mean?

- Time yes. Where in the day would you be? Catherine? Sam?

- Is it morning or afternoon? How would you distinguish between the two?

- What happens to these with the 24-hour clock?

- If Sam sets his alarm clock for 2 o'clock, how many minutes does he have left?

- And how did you work that out?

Chris continued in this vein for almost the whole lesson, gradually drawing out from the class a variety of connections between mathematical representations of number. By the end of the lesson, Chris had developed a network of ideas on the board showing links between length, fractions, time and money using linear and area representations:

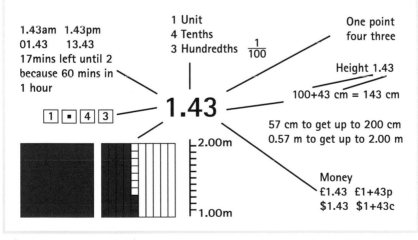

(Swan, 2006, pp. 136–7)

Another strategy for starting with what the learners know might be to let the learners choose where they start when doing exercises from a text book or worksheet. There is little point in starting with simple examples if they can already do them.

Mistakes and misconceptions

As teachers we can find out a great deal about what learners do and do not understand in mathematics from the mistakes they make. Identifying and analysing types of error can help us to diagnose problems and develop strategies to support learners. Effective teaching encourages learners to see mistakes as positive learning opportunities. It is important to develop a mutually supportive atmosphere where learners feel that it is safe to make mistakes and where they are motivated to find out why something did not work.

Mistakes

There are many different kinds of mistakes in mathematics. Learners may choose the wrong operation, make calculation errors, do things in the wrong sequence, muddle procedures. They may not read something carefully, or may misunderstand or misinterpret language, or use notation wrongly.

Misconceptions

Some errors, on the other hand, may indicate conceptual confusion which the teacher needs to help the learner to address. Misconceptions are usually reasoned ways of thinking, they are not random wrong answers. They often arise from over-generalising a rule, for example:

- If 10% = 1/10, then 20% = 1/20
- To multiply by 10 you add a zero
- Multiplying makes numbers bigger
- If you increase the perimeter you increase the area
- The more digits a number has, the bigger it is
- 32 is an odd number because 3 is odd

The aim should be to expose these and deal with them explicitly, rather than trying to avoid having them happen at all. Questions which cause 'cognitive conflict' in the learner create a realisation that something about their understanding needs to be changed. For example, 'multiple representation' activities may lead a learner to realise that 0.345 is smaller than 0.4, even though it has more digits. Cards showing these numbers represented as areas, and on a number line, bring about a re-conceptualisation of decimal place value. Such an approach leads to learning which is deeper and more long lasting than approaches which try to explain the right way.

Teachers need to be aware of common misconceptions, and ensure that activities include questions which will reveal them. For example, in an activity to match fractions and decimals, a teacher might deliberately include, say, 1/4 and 0.25 as well as 1.4 and 2/5. Learners' responses here may reveal how they are thinking, and the task itself should help them to question their own assumptions and to think further.

However, research has shown that the issues around misconceptions are many and complex. Misconceptions can sometimes be hard to distinguish from mistakes, and even harder to deal with and resolve. This takes experience and training, preferably involving peer observation and discussion.

Organisation of classes: Group work and collaborative learning

The rationale for collaborative learning is that people learn mathematics better by sharing knowledge, exploring each other's strategies and bouncing ideas off each other. They learn to make their thinking visible and to listen to each other when they have to explain their reasoning, justify their strategies and answers. Thinking aloud consolidates their understanding, and also involves learning to use appropriate language.

Working together on solutions often means that learners can tackle harder problems than they might do on their own. In joint problem-solving learners are more likely to estimate and develop checking strategies because they are discussing the work. Well-managed group work can be a very effective way of building confidence, developing independence, and can be highly motivating. It encourages learners to make connections with what they know already, offers lots of opportunity for creativity and can enable less confident learners to contribute more than they might in a large group. It can also be a very positive and productive way of managing a wide range of ability.

However, just putting learners into groups does not mean that collaborative group work will automatically take place. Research has uncovered some misunderstandings of the term. For instance, some teachers feel that group work simply involves arranging the class into groups. The learners may be sitting together but still working independently. Some learners are also content to remain 'passengers' and not become too involved in making decisions. It is important to recognise a clear difference between working *in* a group and working *as* a group, and while learners might be seen to be cooperating and enjoying themselves, they are not necessarily collaborating in the sense of

"It is important to recognise a clear difference between working *in* a group and working *as* a group."

working jointly and sharing ideas to solve problems. Real collaborative work involves 'exploratory talk' where decisions are challenged and/or justified, and alternative ideas are proffered and built upon. Similarly, teachers may think learners are having discussions even when the teacher (or one learner) is taking the lead, dominating, showing, or telling other learners how to think.

In collaborative group work discussion is reciprocal and involves shared reasoning. The task itself needs to be designed so that the learners need to work together, and the learners may also need to learn how to work together, listen and share ideas and responsibilities.

Teachers will often need to explain to learners *why* they were adopting such practices, and *how* they should work and learn collaboratively. It is not going to happen overnight, and it is our view that learners need just as much induction, guidance and/or training about how to collaborate together as teachers do. For group work to be effective, clear ground rules need to be in place. Learners can participate in agreeing these so they see the relevance and own them.

Ground rules

- Everyone in the group should take part.
- Talk one at a time, take turns.
- Share ideas and listen to each other.
- Respect each other's opinions.
- Justify your reasoning to the rest of the group.
- Try to follow on from what the last person said.
- Ask others in the group to explain if you don't understand.
- Challenge people if you disagree with them.
- Don't worry about making mistakes.
- Try to find out ways of checking work before asking the teacher.
- Share responsibility for reporting back on the task.

The teacher's role in managing group work is essentially to listen and observe, and to try not to step in and intervene too much. It's critical to give learners space and time to work things out themselves.

There is no hard and fast way of organising classes into groups and it will often depend on the purpose of the session. Although learners can organise themselves into friendship groups, sometimes teachers will need to take the lead by structuring groups either by ability/competence where learners are matched in equal partnership, or by deliberately asking learners of different abilities to work together.

Research tells us that learners enjoy the experience of working in groups; they feel less vulnerable and more relaxed when they worked towards making a group decision. They can also feel that they learn from each other, particularly when they need to explain their thinking.

> *It's great because it's like double the brain work.*

> *It helped to talk about it – we each had contributions.*

> *It makes you think from somebody's point of view.*

> *I like to notice what they [the other learners] can do and what I can do, and put them together and maybe there is something I cannot do but they can do, or I can do and they cannot do, so we put them together and see what we get.*

Below are some examples of activities that are designed to promote small group discussion.

Tackling an open–ended challenge and comparing methods and strategies:

■ How many people can you fit into this room? How would this number be different for different purposes, such as a party or a lesson? How would you begin to think about the problem?

■ How high is this building? How can we use what we already know to help us find out?

Tacking specific mathematical problems and comparing methods and strategies:

■ How many different ways can you work out 16 x 24? Can you say which method you think is the best and give a reason why?

■ How many cups of tea/coffee are you likely to drink in a lifetime?

Sharing a practical task:

■ Design a questionnaire or survey, collect data and present findings, for example a schedule to carry out a traffic survey, identifying the kind of things you want to find out (such as type of vehicle, colour of vehicle, and so on).

Meeting the needs of all learners

Many numeracy classes will have a wide spread of ability and levels. The range will obviously affect how the class works: too wide a spread can make it very difficult for all the learners to work together, while a narrower range of levels can enable more focused teaching and learning and much more opportunity for collaborative group work and problem solving.

"Just because a learner finds the concept of multiplication difficult one week, does not mean that they will struggle with the concept of symmetry the following week."

The Effective Practice study found that, 'Being flexible and able to use a variety of approaches to accommodate learners' needs' and 'Extending learners beyond their comfort zone' were key elements of an effective lesson. Note that it is important that *all* learners are extended, not just those at higher levels.

Some possible ways of meeting the needs of all learners involve the teacher being aware of and responding to things they know about their learners (their interests, their motivations, their culture, a context which may be meaningful to them), while others are to do with the teaching process (feedback, pace, support, task). In each case it is important to ask whether this method will work for your learners. For example, differentiating by task is where the teacher gives a task at the level appropriate for their learner. However, while this seems obvious, and is generally a sound idea, teachers need to be careful that they do not pre-judge what the learner can do, and deny them the chance to engage with more complex ideas. For example, just because a learner finds the concept of multiplication difficult one week, does not mean that they will struggle with the concept of symmetry the following week.

On the other hand, *differentiation by support*, in which all learners are given the same task, but offered support only when it is needed, avoids the dangers of pre-judging learners. Support can come both from teachers or other learners, or come in terms of resources such as a numberline or a calculator.

Similarly, *differentiation by outcome* offers learners open activities that encourage a variety of possible outcomes and encourage the opportunity to set themselves appropriate challenges. Learners can be asked to respond in different ways to the same task. For example:

- Ask learners to write as many different sums as they can with an answer of 3 (or 0.3 or 1/3).
- Ask learners to express four ways of making a designated number using the operation of addition. Teachers can ask learners not to use the same number more than once – it is up to them. An example of a learner's work on this activity can be seen below, using the number 10.

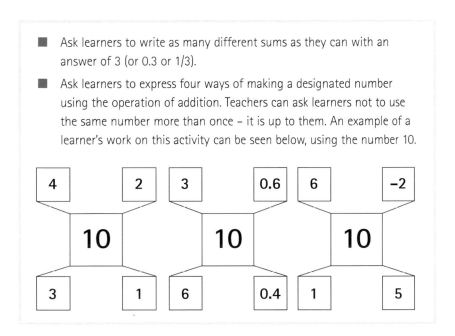

We can see that this activity can give an insight into the learner's thinking and understanding of place value.

Differentiation by pace means giving learners the same activity with the expectation that some will work at different rates and finish at different times.

Assessment

Initial assessment may involve interviewing learners and giving a screening test before they begin a programme of study. *Diagnostic assessment* allows the teacher to get to know a new learner in greater depth. *Formative assessment* helps to enhance learning, and *summative assessment* measures it, it is a summary of what learners have achieved. In other words, summative assessment is *of* learning and formative assessement is *for* learning.

Paul Black and colleagues write that:

> Assessment for learning is any assessment for which the first priority in its design and practice is to serve the purpose of promoting students' learning. It thus differs from assessment designed primarily to serve the purposes of accountability, or of ranking, or of certifying competence. An assessment activity can help learning if it provides information to be used as feedback, by teachers, and by their students, in assessing themselves and each other, to modify the teaching and learning activities in which they are engaged. Such assessment becomes 'formative assessment' when the evidence is actually used to adapt the teaching work to meet learning needs. (Black *et al.*, 2002)

Formative assessment is ongoing and an integral part of the teaching and learning process. It requires teachers to think on their feet, respond flexibly and appropriately, and even change direction within a session. It also requires the active engagement of learners.

Self-assessment and peer assessment

Two areas of formative assessment that Paul Black alludes to, and which are often neglected, are self-assessment and peer assessment. Involving learners in assessment both of their own and each other's work is also a crucial factor in managing their own learning. This enables them to reflect on themselves as thinkers and learners, deepens their understanding of the problems they are working on, encourages them to develop better checking methods, and helps them see how to improve.

Well-designed group tasks provide good opportunities for peer assessment: the tasks will require learners to explain their reasoning to each other, and also to listen, ask questions, criticise, make suggestions and try out solutions.

Questioning

A key part of formative assessment involves teachers asking learners questions. Paul Black writes that, 'The only point of asking questions is to raise issues about which the teacher needs information or about which the students need to think' (Black *et al.*, 2002, p. 7). However, research shows that many numeracy teachers tend to use low-level, closed, factual recall questions more frequently than higher-level, open questions that reveal learners' thinking processes or require learners to use mathematical reasoning.

Teachers need closed questions if they want indicative information about knowledge and understanding – 'Do you know what 3 x 7 is?' or 'What is the area of this triangle?' However, while closed questions can clearly serve a purpose as a learning check, they often do not expose thinking processes, so give little information to the teacher on what to do next. Open questions, on the other hand, can establish the limits of a learner's understanding, what they still need to learn, what misconceptions they might have, and how best to address these. Examples of types of questions are given below.

'Lower–order' closed questions:

Type of question	Example
Asking directly	What is 6 x 4?
Reassuring	Are you OK with that?
Checking (prior knowledge)	Do you know what 'range' means?
Clarifying	Is it one AND a half or one half?
Reminding	Is it always, or sometimes...?
Prompting and guiding	Have you thought about using half a square?

'Higher–order' open questions:

Type of question	Example
Creating examples	Can you show me an example of: ■ an even number? ■ a square number? ■ a fraction which is less than 1/2? ■ a shape with an area of 12 square units ... and another ... and another ...? ■ a shape with an area of 12 square units and a perimeter of 16 units...and another...and another?
Evaluating and correcting	What is wrong with this statement? How could you correct it? ■ When you multiply by 10 you add a nought ■ 2/10+3/10=5/20 ■ All two-digit numbers are even numbers ■ John is 170 metres tall ■ Dividing makes smaller

Type of question	Example
Comparing and organising	What is the same and what is different about: ■ fractions, decimals and percentages? ■ ■ 2 ÷ 4 and 4 ÷ 2
Modifying and changing	How can you change: ■ pence into pounds? ■ metres into centimetres? How could you modify this shape so that it has a line of symmetry?
Generalising and conjecturing	How would you describe these patterns? ■ 3, 6, 9, 12, 15, … ■ 1, 2, 4, 8, 16, 32, … ■ 1, 4, 9, 16, 25, … ■ Are these statements sometimes, always or never true? If sometimes, when exactly? ■ If you add odd numbers together you always get an odd number as your answer. ■ If you add one to the top and bottom of a fraction, it gets bigger in value.
Explaining and justifying	■ Can you give me a reason why a square is also a rectangle? ■ Can you draw a diagram to show why 1/2 is smaller than 3/5? ■ How can you be sure that a triangle can't have two right angles? ■ Can you explain why 0.5 is the same as 1/2?

Further examples of open questions which can be used to probe understanding and explore thinking might be:

- How did you find that out? Can you show how you worked it out? Can you think of any other ways of doing that?

- How could we tackle this problem? Would it help to change the numbers?

- A learner explains something to the group. The teacher then asks other another learner to explain what the first learner said.

- A learner has '7 x 38 = 266'. The teacher says, 'What else could you work out from that statement? Is that the same as '14 x 19'? Can you see any connection? Could you use this idea anywhere else?

- If the answer is 10, what was the question? Can you think of some easy questions and some much more difficult questions to get this answer?

- What would be a really good question to ask about what we have been doing today?

- What was easy and what was difficult in the work today? Why?

Teachers need to develop skills of observation and listening so that learners are given time to think. When teachers are listening to a learner's explanation or answer they are constantly processing the information and thinking 'in the moment' of what to say and do next. This requires a high degree of skill and experience and shows how difficult a teacher's job really is.

Learners also need to be encouraged to ask questions, directed both to the teacher and to each other. As with learning how to work collaboratively and discuss together, learners will also need help in knowing what kind of questions to ask and how to ask them.

Teachers can find it difficult to pause after asking questions so that learners have time to reflect and respond. Research by Paul Black and Dylan Wiliam (1998) found that the average 'wait time' between a teacher asking a question and it being answered (sometime by the teacher themselves) was 0.8 seconds. There are several reasons why teachers have a tendency to 'jump in': some may be afraid of placing learners in a position of discomfort or uncertainty, others will be concerned that the session is going too slowly and learners are losing interest; it is also the case that learners can sometimes put the teacher under pressure to tell them the answer – this might be their expectation of how teachers are supposed to behave.

"Teachers need to develop skills of observation and listening so that learners are given time to think."

A helpful way of ensuring that questions are addressed to all learners in a group is to ask the learners to show their responses on small individual whiteboards, which can be used as versatile 'thinking pads'. These encourage learners to try ideas out, and experiment without feeling anxious about making mistakes.

In conclusion, a key focus for numeracy teachers needs to be framing questions which are

- worth asking;
- explore issues and develop activities; and
- expose thinking as well as deepen and extend learners' understanding.

Follow-up questions are equally important, to

- probe;
- check reasoning; and
- extend learners' understandings.

4 | What next?

Our research has shown that there is already much good practice in adult numeracy classrooms. It is clear that the process of reflecting on beliefs and practice is essential to developing as a teacher. However, effective practice is not something for which there is a recipe. The activities presented in this guide have worked for others, and may work for you. You may find the following suggestions useful:

- Do not look for any 'magic bullets' in teaching numeracy. If these existed it would not be the difficult job we know it to be.

- Improve on what already works well, and explore new ideas by working with another teacher to plan together and observe each other teaching.

- Do not try to change too much in one go – you could start by simply writing down a few good questions based on the misconceptions you think your learners may have.

- Just because you teach something do not assume it has been learned. Your learners will need time for discussion, and access to rich activities to develop deep understanding of mathematical ideas. Your role is to uncover misconceptions and provide activities to challenge learners to new ways of thinking.

- If something does not work, do not give up. Ask yourself if it went wrong, or if it just went differently. Our research shows that teachers sometimes think an activity failed when in fact the learners found it useful. Ask them, and then maybe persist with the new activity.

- Encourage learners to think and to talk about their thinking.

- Encourage your learners to work collaboratively – that is as a group, not simply in a group. Do not allow any passengers – encourage all learners to participate.

- Do not protect your learners from intellectual challenge – the aim is to help them become functional mathematical problem solvers. Confidence comes from responding to challenges, not from doing things which are well within their comfort zone.

- Understand what motivates your learners in joining numeracy classes, and build on it.

■ Do not pre-judge what your learners know or can do, or at what pace they can work. Initial tests can only be indicative at best. The teachers on the TTM project found their learners often knew much more than they imagined.

■ Further support for all of the above:

  The Collaborative Professional Development sessions, and the teaching and learning sessions within the Thinking Through Mathematics: strategies for teaching and learning ring binder (available at **http://www.Maths4Life.org**).

  After trying some of the professional development and teaching activities in Thinking Through Mathematics, you are encouraged to contribute to improving practice through collaboration by sharing your experiences on the National Centre for Excellence in the Teaching of Mathematics website (**http://www.ncetm.org.uk**).

  Maths4Life has produced a series of booklets which aim to give classroom ideas on a range of topics: *Fractions*; *Topic-Based Teaching*; *Number*; *Time and Money*; and *Measurement*.

Bibliography

Ahmed, A. (1987) *Better Mathematics: A Curriculum Development Study*. London: HMSO.

Askew, M., Brown, M., Rhodes, V., Wiliam, D. and Johnson, D. (1997) *Effective Teachers of Numeracy*. London: King's College London.

Askew, M. and Wiliam, D. (1995) *Recent Research in Mathematics Education 5–16*. London: HMSO.

Black, P. and Wiliam, D. (1998). *Inside the Black Box : Raising Standards Through Classroom Assessment*. London: King's College, London School of Education.

Black, P., Harrison, C., Lee, C., Marshall, B. and William, D. (2002) *Working Inside the Black Box: Assessment for Learning in the Classroom*. London: nferNelson.

Coben, D., Brown, M., Rhodes, V., Swain, J., Ananiadou, K. and Brown, P. (2007) *Effective Teaching and Learing: Numeracy*. London: NRDC.

DfEE (1999) *A Fresh Start: Improving Literacy and Numeracy*. The report of the Working Group chaired by Claus Moser. London: Department for Education and Employment.

DfES (2005) 14–19 *Education and Skills*. London: Department for Education and Skills.

Ecclestone, K. (2002) *Formative Assessment in Lifelong Learning*. London: Routledge.

Ecclestone, K. (2002) *Learning Autonomy in Post-16 Education*. London: Taylor and Francis.

Newmarch, B. (2005) *Developing Numeracy, Supporting Achievement*. Leicester: NIACE.

NRDC (n.d.) Project on formative assessment. At: **http://www.nrdc.org.uk/projects_details.asp?ProjectID=33**

Ofsted (2006) *Evaluating Mathematics Provision for 14–19 Year-Olds*. London: HMSO. At: **http://www.ofsted.gov.uk/publications**

QCA (2006) *Functional Skills Standards: Mathematics.* London: Qualifications and Curriculum Authority.

Smith, A. (2004) *Making Mathematics Count. Report of Enquiry into Post-14 Mathematics Education.* London: Department for Education and Skills.

Swain, J., Baker, E., Holder, D., Newmarch, B. and Coben, D. (2005) *'Beyond the Daily Application': Making Numeracy Teaching Meaningful to Adult Learners.* London: NRDC.

Swain, J. and Swan, M. (2007) *Thinking Through Mathematics: A Research Report.* London: NRDC.

Swan, M. (2005). *Improving Learning in Mathematics: Challenges and Strategies.* Sheffield: Teaching and Learning Division, Department for Education and Skills' Standards Unit.

Swan, M. (2006). *Collaborative Learning in Mathematics: A Challenge to our Beliefs and Practices.* Leicester: NIACE; London: NRDC.

Tomlin, A., Coben, D., Baxter, M., Wresniwiro, T., Leddy, E. and Richards, L. (2006) *Measurement Was Not Taught When They Built the Pyramids – Was It? The Teaching and Learning of Common Measures in Adult Numeracy.* London: NRDC.